GRASSLAND

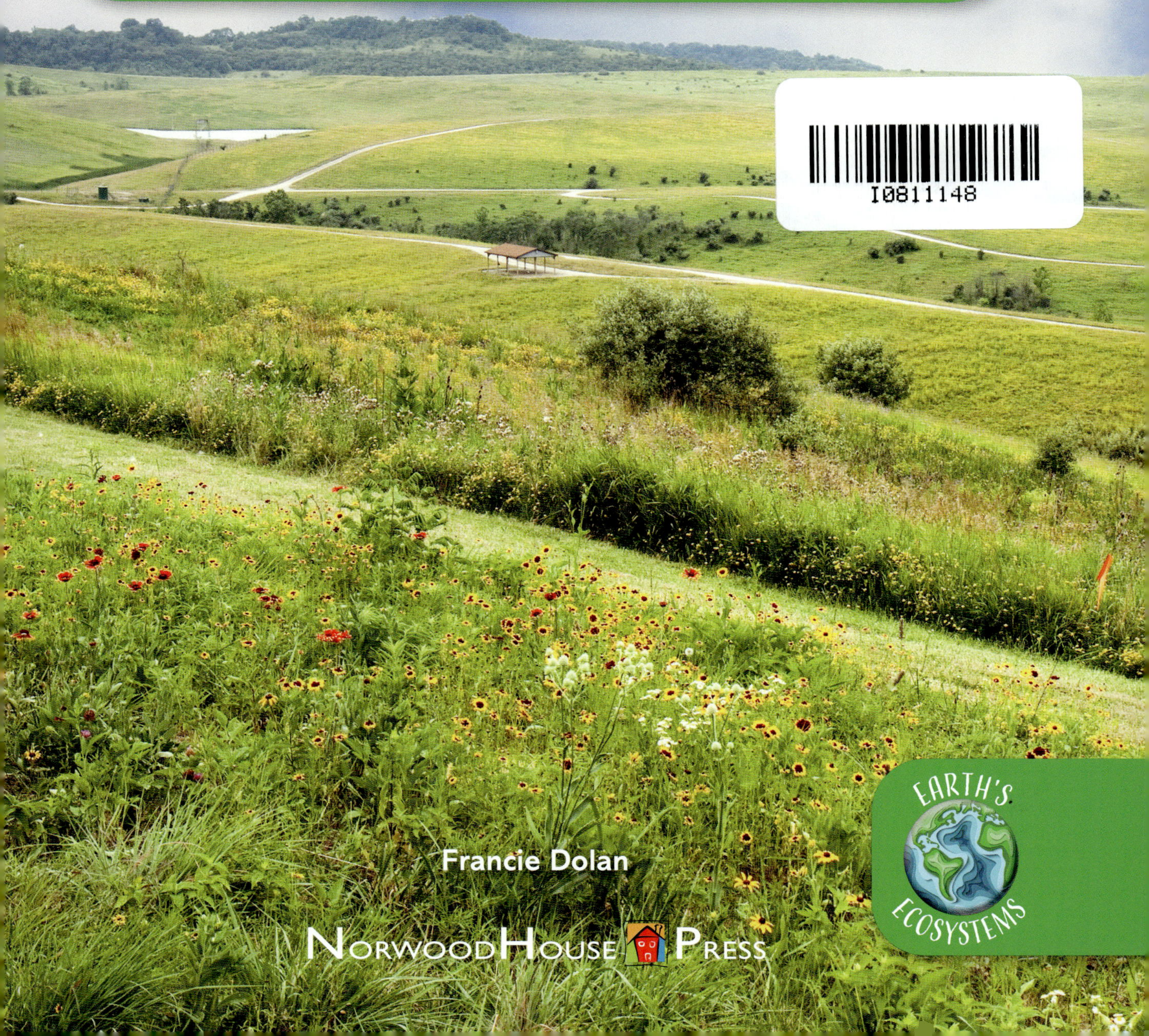

EARTH'S ECOSYSTEMS

Francie Dolan

NORWOODHOUSE PRESS

Cataloging-in-Publication Data

Names: Dolan, Francie.
Title: Grassland / Francie Dolan.
Description: Buffalo, NY : Norwood House Press, 2026. | Series: Earth's ecosystems | Includes glossary and index.
Identifiers: ISBN 9781978576988 (pbk.) | ISBN 9781978576995 (library bound) | ISBN 9781978577008 (ebook)
Subjects: LCSH: Grassland ecology--Juvenile literature. | Grassland animals--Juvenile literature.
Classification: LCC QH541.5.P7 D65 2026 | DDC 577.4--dc23

Published in 2026 by
Norwood House Press
2544 Clinton Street
Buffalo, NY 14224

Designer: Rhea Magaro
Editor: Kim Thompson

Photo credits:Cover, p. 1 Ami Parikh, Kumer Oksana/Shutterstock.com; p. 3 Dmitry Fch/Shutterstock.com; p. 5 Sergei Mishchenko/Shutterstock.com; p. 6 Olga.Sh/Shutterstock.com; p. 7 Roger de la Harpe/Shutterstock.com; p. 9 Matauw/Shutterstock.com; p. 10 LedyX/Shutterstock.com; p. 11 Duan Wade/Shutterstock.com; p. 12 Gonzalo Buzonni/Shutterstock.com; p. 13 Alexandr T/Shutterstock.com; p. 14 Try_my_best/Shutterstock.com; pp. 15, 19 Dennis Laughlin/Shutterstock.com; p. 16 Jurgens Potgieter/Shutterstock.com; p. 18 Frank Goma, Mariola Anna S /Shutterstock.com; p. 19 Annette Shaff/ Shutterstock.com; p. 20 CLOUD-WALKER/Shutterstock.com; p. 21 Bogdan Kovenkin/Shutterstock.com

Printed in the United States of America

TABLE OF CONTENTS

The Grassland Ecosystem

Eco- means "home" or "environment." *System* means "a group of things that work together." Earth has many **ecosystems** that support life. Each is home to a network of living things that depend on each other.

One kind of ecosystem is a grassland. Grasslands make up at least one-quarter of Earth's land. In different places, they may be called prairies, **steppes**, or **savannas**.

Grasslands are large, open areas with low-growing plants. Most are hot in summer and cold in winter.

Few trees grow. Grasslands get more rain than **deserts**, but they do not get enough rain to support forests.

Grassland Plants

Thousands of grass **species** grow in grasslands. Some types are purple needlegrass, wild oats, foxtail, and ryegrass.

Grasses have long, deep roots. They keep soil in place and help prevent **erosion**. When fire sweeps across the land, grasses are protected. Because their stems and buds grow underground, they quickly regrow.

Wildflowers grow in grasslands. You might find asters, blazing stars, goldenrod, sunflowers, and wild indigo.

Wildflowers attract butterflies and other insects. Their seeds provide food for birds and other animals. In spring, their blooms cover the land with color.

Grassland Animals

The Eurasian Steppe is one of the largest grasslands on Earth. Przewalski's horses roam there.

Like other **ungulates**, these wild horses have **adaptations** that help them survive in grasslands. Eyes on the sides of their heads let them see predators far across the grassland. **Hooves** help them run fast. Their stomachs are able to digest tough grass.

In grasslands, there is nowhere to hide. Animals are exposed to the weather and to predators. Some, like the prairie dog, burrow underground.

Prairie dogs have strong legs and claws for digging. They make complex tunnel networks called towns. All the animals in a prairie dog town protect each other.

Grassland predators cannot attack from behind big trees or rocks. **Camouflage** lets them hide in plain sight. The cheetah's spotted coat helps it blend into the tall grass.

Grassland Food Chains

In a grassland, living things eat other living things in food chains. A grasshopper might feed on wild indigo. A prairie dog may eat the grasshopper.

A badger may catch and eat the prairie dog. After the badger dies, a coyote may **scavenge** on its remains.

Many grassland food chains together form a food web. It shows how all living things in a grassland ecosystem depend on each other for survival.

GRASSLAND FOOD WEB

Glossary

adaptations (ad-ap-TAY-shuhns): physical or behavioral changes that help plants and animals survive in their environment

camouflage (KAM-uh-flahzh): a disguise or natural coloring that lets animals hide by making them look like their surroundings

deserts (DEZ-urts): very dry ecosystems that get less than 10 inches (25 centimeters) of rain each year

ecosystems (EE-koh-sis-tuhms): natural communities where plants, animals, and their environment all work together

erosion (i-ROH-zhuhn): the wearing away of something, such as soil or rock, by water or wind

hooves (huvz): the hard parts on the feet of some animals like horses, cows, and zebras

savannas (suh-VAN-uhz): grasslands in tropical places on Earth such as Africa, South America, and India

scavenge (SKAV-uhnj): to look for and eat food that is already dead

species (SPEE-sheez): a group of living things that are alike and can reproduce together

steppes (steps): grasslands in places on Earth that have temperate climates such as Asia and Europe

ungulates (UHN-gyuh-lets): mammals that have four legs and hooves, including antelope, elephants, rhinos, and bison

Thinking Questions

1. What is an ecosystem?
2. Describe a grassland.
3. Give an example of an adaptation that helps grassland plants survive.
4. Give an example of an adaptation that helps grassland animals survive.
5. What does a food chain show?

Index

About the Author

Francie Dolan is continually amazed by the natural world and how Earth's plants, animals, and natural resources are interconnected. From her home near Seattle, Washington, she loves to hike and explore forests, lakes, mountains, and the seashore. When she gets home, she likes to draw and write about what she sees on her adventures.